THE PRACTICAL STRATEGIES SERIES
IN GIFTED EDUCATION

series editors
FRANCES A. KARNES & KRISTEN R. STEPHENS

Enrichment Opportunities for Gifted Learners

Julia L. Roberts

Routledge
Taylor & Francis Group

NEW YORK AND LONDON

First published 2005 by Prufrock Press Inc.

Published 2021 by Routledge
605 Third Avenue, New York, NY 10017
2 Park Square, Milton Park, Abingdon, Oxon OX14 4RN

Routledge is an imprint of the Taylor & Francis Group, an informa business

ISBN 13: 978-1-59363-020-1 (pbk)

Contents

The Practical Strategies Series in Gifted Education offers teachers, counselors, administrators, parents, and other interested parties with up-to-date instructional techniques and information on a variety of issues pertinent to the field of gifted education. Each guide addresses a focused topic and is written by scholars with authority on the issue. Several guides have been published. Among the titles are:

- *Acceleration Strategies for Teaching Gifted Learners*
- *Curriculum Compacting: An Easy Start to Differentiating for High-Potential Students*
- *Enrichment Opportunities for Gifted Learners*
- *Independent Study for Gifted Learners*
- *Motivating Gifted Students*
- *Questioning Strategies for Teaching the Gifted*
- *Social & Emotional Teaching Strategies*
- *Using Media & Technology With Gifted Learners*

For a current listing of available guides within the series, please contact Prufrock Press at (800) 998-2208 or visit http://www.prufrock.com.

To enrich or not to enrich has often been the question. This question becomes increasingly important at a time when the major emphasis in many classrooms and schools is on mastering basic skills and core content at grade level. Enrichment opportunities are thus essential for those students who have already mastered the basic material. Educators who want all students to learn new things each day know it is imperative to offer enrichment opportunities to those who can demonstrate they already know most or all of what is being taught. Equity is offering learning experiences matched to needs, interests, and abilities; it is not offering the same learning opportunities to all children of the same age on the same time schedule. Life should be filled with enriching experiences that ensure that all children, including those who are gifted and talented, make continuous progress.

Enrichment is necessary because children differ. Even children born on the same day of the same year have different needs, interests, and abilities. For those who are gifted and talented, many of their needs are the result of their strengths. Strengths create the need for enrichment opportunities; and, if their identified strengths are to be enhanced, students must have opportunities to learn above and beyond what is expected for others their age. A child may be above grade level in all content areas or in only one. Even those who are gifted and talented differ considerably, so what is enriching for one may not be so for another.

Services for the gifted and talented need to include learning experiences with enrichment and acceleration opportunities. Some of these services will combine enrichment with acceleration in order to provide appropriate learning experiences for those students who are ready for more challenging opportunities to learn. Enrichment and acceleration are discrete services that work well in combination. The old question of whether it is better to accelerate or to enrich is meaningless, as students often need a combination of the two. The gifted and talented need to learn at a faster pace with more complex content; they need a rich curriculum with various opportunities that start with what they know and can already do.

The stakes are high for schools and communities when they plan to provide appropriate learning opportunities for those students who are ready for advanced learning. In an age of accountability, schools will increase their success on assessment when all children are learning at the highest levels possible. Otherwise, some children, including the gifted and talented, will be left behind. Providing appropriately challenging learning experiences, nurturing interests, and developing strengths yield citizens who can provide leadership in all areas of human endeavor, including space exploration, medical research, the visual and performing arts, and politics.

What Is Enrichment?

Enrichment describes experiences inside and outside the classroom that provide opportunities to learn above and beyond what is usually provided at a particular grade level. Enrichment is defined by *Webster's Dictionary* as making something rich or richer, especially by the addition or increase of some desirable quality, attribute, or ingredient.

Renzulli and Reis (1997) described enrichment as learning activities that are "designed to encourage creative productivity on the part of young people by exposing them to various topics, areas of interest, and fields of study and to further train them to apply advanced content, process-training skills, and methodology training to self-selected areas of interest" (p. 14). Schiever and Maker (2003) stated, "The goal of an enrichment program is to offer curriculum that is greater in depth or breadth than that generally provided; that is, to challenge and offer growth in the area of the student's giftedness" (p. 164). According to Coleman and Cross (2001), "Enrichment is a broad term used to refer to program organization that extends, supplements, and sometimes replaces aspects of the school's structure. In its broadest interpretation, enrichment encompasses a number of modifications in standard educational practices" (p. 298).

For this publication, the term *enrichment* refers to modifications a teacher makes to go above or beyond the regular curriculum for a student or a cluster of students who need advanced learning opportunities, and it includes programs or services that spark interests and develop skills and expertise both within the school and beyond in the local or broader community.

Enrichment comes in many configurations and can be delivered as various services to students. What they all have in common is that they offer opportunities to engage the learner beyond what is traditionally available at a particular grade level. Some configurations offer enrichment to one child, a pair of students, a cluster of children, or a class that has been grouped by interests, needs, and abilities.

Enrichment provides students with opportunities to extend learning. There are three primary purposes for enrichment: fostering interest; nurturing talent, developing expertise, or both; and increasing achievement. Enrichment opportunities may address one, two, or all three of these purposes.

Reason 1: Fostering Interest

How do students discover possibilities relating to an idea or a field of study? Where do they find interests about which they may become passionate?

The first step in nurturing an interest is having an experience with the topic. That experience may be firsthand, or it may be the result of reading, attending a lecture or presentation, or learning about a topic, career, or special interest in a myriad of ways. Since various enrichment opportunities are planned by teachers, parents, and the students themselves, it is important to view enrichment as occurring in classrooms, in extracurricular activities sponsored by the schools, and in the community and beyond.

Reason 2: Nurturing Talent, Developing Expertise, or Both

How do students move to the next level in their talent area? How do they acquire expertise in an area of interest?

Of course, a partial answer to these questions depends upon the individual's passion to move to the next level of talent or expertise and his or her willingness to work hard to do so. Attending outstanding performances of talent and interacting with experts provide models for young people interested in a particular area. As students learn from professionals who are experts, they find stimulating ideas to pursue. Just imagine the benefits to a young person who conducts research alongside a specialist in her field of expertise or learns music from a professional who can share his passion for a particular instrument.

> *Harriet O'Malley, my junior high school art teacher, was my inspiration for pursuing an art career. She recognized the talent that I took for granted and contacted my mom so that she could stay on top of me. Drawing and painting were second nature to me. Early on, she took me under her wing and helped me to further my talent as a young artist. Without her involvement, I doubt that I would have become the artist that I am today.*

—Ed Hamilton,
nationally known sculptor

Reason 3: Increasing Achievement

How do students increase their achievement in a content area in which they are already way ahead of their agemates?

Without appropriate learning opportunities both in and outside of school, children may not achieve at the level that equates to their potential. This gap between achievement and potential is truly an achievement gap that cannot be tolerated. Eliminating this achievement gap will benefit both the individual and the community—local, state, national, and global. The U.S. Commission on National Security for the 21st Century noted in its report *Road Map for National Security: Imperative for Change* (2001):

> The scale and nature of the ongoing revolution in science and technology, and what this implies for the quality of human capital in the 21st century, pose critical national security challenges for the United States. Second only to a weapon of mass destruction detonating in an American city, we can think of nothing more dangerous than a failure to manage properly science, technology, and education for the common good over the next quarter century. . . . The capacity of America's educational system to create a 21st century workforce second to none in the world is a national security issue of the first order. As things stand, this country is forfeiting that capacity. (pp. 30, 38)

This gap between opportunities to learn and achievement potential can be seen in all content and talent areas. The gap is the widest when the teacher believes that grade level achievement is the goal for all children in that classroom for the year. Strategies to eliminate the achievement gap for those who are gifted and talented will certainly include enrichment.

Who Offers Enrichment?

Educators

Throughout a child's school experience, educators are responsible for providing enrichment opportunities for those who demonstrate the need to learn above and beyond the regular curriculum.

Teachers are the ones who preassess what students know and are able to do in relation to unit objectives and then design learning experiences to challenge those who are ready for more advanced learning. Educators are involved in enrichment throughout the school day and with extracurricular activities. Teachers, counselors, and administrators gather information about the needs and interests of their students in order to tap into and spark their interests and develop their talents. Assessing interests often leads to the development of new clubs or interest groups, as well as making modifications to the curriculum.

Leaders in Organizations

Most communities have various organizations in which young people can become involved. Adults in the community provide leadership in Boy Scouts, Girl Scouts, 4-H Club, theater groups, community choirs, and a variety of other opportunities. Leaders of these organizations may be volunteers or professionals; they may be retired teachers, university or college students, business and industry personnel, or artists and musicians. The key to continued leadership is finding the right expertise and leadership qualities to complement organizational goals.

Personnel in University Programs

Colleges, universities, and community colleges have personnel who may be interested in offering enrichment opportunities. Institutions of higher education are ideal locations for enrichment because they have the equipment and facilities that encourage exploration of new areas for learning and they have faculty members with expertise in a variety of content areas. Some universities have organizations that sponsor enrichment programs for elementary, middle, and high schools students. For example, they may have a center for gifted education or gifted studies. If enrichment programs are not being offered by a local institution of higher education, a group of parents or educators may schedule a meeting with the president or provost to discuss the possibility of working together to offer enrichment programs.

Private Teachers

Private teachers may be teachers in public or private schools, university personnel, artists and musicians, or experts. As a student's talent and expertise increase, it is extremely important to have a teacher who can take him or her to the next level. Private teachers are most frequently used with music, dance, and art lessons, but they are equally important for offering experiences in higher level science, mathematics, foreign language, or writing. The key to using a private teacher successfully to provide enrichment is matching the child's interests and level of achievement to the teacher's expertise and experience in talent development.

Parents

Parents can provide enrichment both in and outside of school. In school, parents can get Junior Great Books training and lead discussion groups. They may volunteer to lead Odyssey of the Mind or other academic teams. They can share their expertise related to their own career or interests with students through presentations, interactive sessions, and mentoring. Outside of school, parents can organize enrichment studies for their child or other children with similar interests. These enrichment studies could focus on a foreign language, artistic studies, literacy circles, or any other topic of interest.

Who Should Receive Enrichment?

Every student should enjoy ongoing opportunities to learn from a high-quality curriculum that is taught using a variety of strategies. All students need curricula that are motivating in terms of content, process, and product. All need to receive instruction that is well planned and engaging. Of course, every child must be considered when planning the curriculum—from children who are not yet at grade level to those who are performing above grade level.

For all students to make continuous progress, the learning ceiling must be removed. Those performing beyond grade level must have enrichment options built into their curriculum in order to continue learning and reach their potential. Some students need enrichment in one content area, while others will require enrichment in all areas. Every student who demonstrates mastery of any part of the regular curriculum needs enrichment opportunities that extend, replace, or supplement the curriculum. Educators must document the need for learning that extends beyond the regular curriculum and know that enrichment is not a reward given to some children, but a response to need. Unfortunately, gifted children's needs are often overlooked because they are the result of strengths, rather than deficiencies.

Creating a culture that values learning is an important goal. Students who are engaged in ongoing, challenging learning experiences will develop into lifelong learners. *Prisoners of Time* (1994), the report of the National Education Commission on Time and Learning, vividly emphasized the tremendous importance of learning when it stated, "The strongest message this Commission can send to the American people is that education must become a new national obsession as powerful as sports and entertainment, if we are to avoid a spiral of economic and social decline" (p. 3).

What happens to students who are in need of enrichment, but do not receive it? Contrary to the commonly held myth that "gifted children will make it on their own," the casualties are numerous.

As an education writer and a long-time mentor to disadvantaged youths, I used to buy into the idea that it was elitist to advocate for gifted students. I believed, as many people still do, that highly intelligent children would do well in any educational environment, that they were almost hard-wired for academic success. As a parent of a gifted child, I found out how wrong I was.

Providing enrichment for gifted students is not only critical to their emotional and intellectual development, but it is one of the country's most important educational equity issues. Most schools and school districts do not serve gifted students well. They fail to use broad methods of identifying giftedness and fail to provide adequate training and resources to help teachers make appropriate modifications in the classrooms.

My child has been a barometer of those inconsistent practices. I have seen him soar when talented teachers ignited his love of learning and guided him through unlimited discover-

ies. Sadly, I also have seen his interest in school fade when confronted with seemingly endless terms of low-level, repetitive instruction.

We can do better for our brightest children. We must.

—Holly Holland,
parent

What Are Strategies for Offering Enrichment in Classrooms?

What key elements must be inherent in an enrichment experience, whether it be for one student, a cluster of students, or a class full of students who are all ready for enrichment?

First, the experience must take the curriculum deeper or wider for those who are ready to extend their learning. Second, enrichment must provide opportunities for students to have learning experiences that match their interests, needs, and abilities, realizing that one size does not fit all. Third, enrichment must open opportunity to learn and remove the learning ceiling for those who are ready for more academic challenge. Finally, it must be engaging and motivate students to work hard to achieve at high levels.

Differentiation

Differentiation is one of the hottest topics in education in the 21st century. Educators and parents know that all children of the same age or grade are not at the same achievement level in math, language arts, science, social studies, or the visual and performing arts. Consequently, it is necessary to offer different learning experiences to match readiness and achievement, as well as to spark interest. Differentiation is a form of enrichment, as it provides opportunities for students to study the same core content at levels that go above and beyond the grade-level curriculum.

To differentiate in a classroom is more than having students engage in a variety of learning experiences. Differentiation matches experiences to learn above or beyond the regular curriculum to the students' interests, needs, and levels of achievement. Differentiation is done with the purpose of addressing the learning level of each child, thus, removing the learning ceiling. The following are some guiding questions for differentiation:

1.   What do I want students to know or be able to do?

2.   Who already knows the information or can do it?

3.   What can I do for the students so they can make continuous progress and extend their learning?

Preassessment

Meaningful learning experiences that are differentiated begin with preassessment. The preassessment tells what the student knows about the unit of study before it is taught. Preassessment documents whether a student is or is not ready for more advanced learning experiences. The results guide the teacher in planning which experiences will match the student's level of content knowledge in relationship to the unit objectives, as well as his or her interests and learning preferences. Although some educators may think that it is best to give every student the same opportunity to learn (and they define "same opportunity" as identical learning experiences), learning is optimized for each child when it allows him or her to make continuous progress. Targeting learning experience to preassessment results makes learning efficient and raises the level of achievement of all students, including those who are gifted and talented. Preassessment makes differentiation defensible, as the teacher has documentation of the need for differentiated learning experiences.

Preassessment may take many forms. For example, it may be the end-of-the-unit test that the teacher administers prior to beginning the unit in order to direct the selection of learning experiences. Students who demonstrate that they already know most or all of what the teacher is planning to teach will gain time for studying the topic in greater depth through differentiated learning experiences. What form the preassessment takes is not nearly as important as the fact that it allows the teacher to document what students have already learned, thus justifying having one or more students engage in alternate learning experiences.

> *The pretest is the map for instruction. The formative tests are the detours. The posttesting is the determination of how successful we are in finding the final destination. I tell my children that I don't want them "running in one spot over and over" like a cartoon character may do. I want them running and jumping into new adventures all the time.*

> —Patrice McCrary,
> kindergarten teacher
> and 2003 Kentucky Teacher of the Year

Content, Process, and Product

Each and every student deserves the opportunity to learn new things in school on an ongoing basis. Students need learning experiences that are challenging if they are to improve their abilities to think and learn. Students need challenging material to study (content), engaging points of inquiry (process), and interesting ways to show what has been learned (products). It is the combination of content, process, and product that makes a learning experience (see Figure 1).

Planning a unit of study begins with determining the *content* or topic to be studied; in other words, answering the following question: What does the teacher want the students to learn?

The core content is the starting point for planning most units. How can a teacher differentiate or enrich the content for a child who has mastered most of the core content in the unit? The differentiated or enriched content must be related to the core content, but it will be more complex and abstract. The content also becomes more complex when it addresses problems and issues related to the core content.

For example, if a student has shown mastery or near mastery of the key concepts in a solar system unit, then he or she

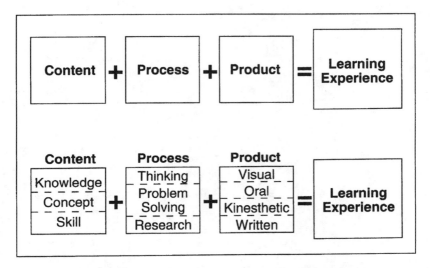

Figure 1. Elements of learning experiences

Note. From "Writing Units That Remove the Learning Ceiling" (p. 225), by J. L. Roberts & R. A. Roberts, in F. A. Karnes & S. M. Bean (Eds.), *Methods and Materials for Teaching the Gifted*, 2001, Waco, TX: Prufrock Press. Copyright ©2001 by Prufrock Press. Reprinted with permission.

may explore the possible impact on Earth of an asteroid hitting the moon or, using the new information about Mars, design a space station for humans. There is no limit to the depth of most concepts that are taught in elementary, middle, and high school classes. In fact, most concepts are the topics of graduate courses.

An equally important aspect in planning learning experiences is the *process*. Process focuses on what the teacher wants the students to do cognitively. Kanevsky (2003) stated, "Tiering means the most capable students will be given more complex versions of an assignment and they'll be expected to complete it in the same amount of time as students who need simpler versions of the activity and more support" (p. 42). She suggested using Venn diagrams to design learning experiences that are tiered to make the process more challenging for those students who are ready to advance. The complexity increases with the number of circles in the Venn diagram. Three tasks illustrate how the Venn diagram can be used to examine

Leaders During War Years

Task 1: Describe the leadership style
of Wilson or Roosevelt.

Figure 2. Task 1 of tiered assignment

Presidential leadership during wartime (see Figures 2, 3, and 4).

The *product* is the way students will show what they have learned. Products can be categorized in various ways. Curry and Samara (1994) used the categories of visual, oral, kinesthetic, and written, while Karnes and Stephens (2000) specified oral, written, visual, performance, and multicategorical. The key to offering product choice and variety is that some products are more interesting to some students; consequently, the right product will motivate students to work hard to achieve at high levels. Some products offer the potential to learn new skills and to have up-to-date means of communicating with an audience. For example, the assignment to give a speech could be enhanced with the addition of the opportunity to do so with a PowerPoint presentation.

A straightforward way to design learning experiences that can be used to differentiate is to do so on the Differentiated Learning Experiences Form (see Figures 5 and 6).

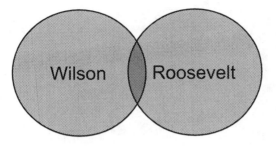

Leaders During War Years

Task 2: In what ways were these two leaders alike and different in their leadership?

Figure 3. Task 2 of tiered assignment

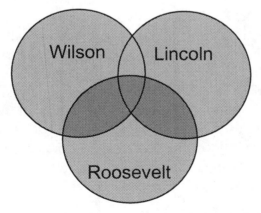

Leaders During War Years

Task 3: In what ways were these three leaders alike and different in their leadership?

Figure 4. Task 3 of tiered assignment

PLANNING FOR DIFFERENTIATED LEARNING EXPERIENCES

PROCESS/VERB	CONCEPT/IDEA	PRODUCT
EVALUATION		
SYNTHESIS		
ANALYSIS		
APPLICATION		
COMPREHENSION		
KNOWLEDGE		

Figure 5. Differentiated learning experiences form

PLANNING FOR DIFFERENTIATED LEARNING EXPERIENCES

	PROCESS/VERB	CONCEPT/IDEA	PRODUCT
EVALUATION	Justify	Fractions	Persuasive Essay or Debate
	Justify learning about fractions in a debate or a persuasive essay.		
SYNTHESIS	Design	Fractions	Game
	Design a game that teaches about fractions		
ANALYSIS	Compare	Fractions	Venn Diagram
	Compare fractions and decimals on a Venn Diagram.		
APPLICATION	Organize	Fractions	Numberline
	Organize fractions on a numberline.		
COMPREHENSION	Explain	Fractions	Discussion or Role Play
	Explain fractions in a discussion or a role play.		
KNOWLEDGE	Identify	Fractions	Chart or Pictures
	Identify fractions on a chart or with pictures.		

Figure 6. Example of a completed
differentiated learning experiences form

Planning With Your Students to Maximize Enrichment Experiences

In order to get the most out of an enrichment opportunity, students must have an interest that is incorporated into the enrichment experience. Initial opportunities may be planned to see if there is an interest or to create one. If a student is interested, then he or she will soar with the opportunity if it is matched to his or her level of expertise.

Outside of school, it is also important to assess the readiness of the student for the enrichment opportunity. Does the student have the prerequisite skills to participate successfully in the enrichment opportunity? This question is key to getting the most out of the experience. Enrichment should allow the student to continue learning. Certainly, it is important that the student wants to be involved in the experience and that he or she is at a level of skill and knowledge needed for success when entering the extracurricular experience.

Strategies for maximizing the enrichment experiences include goal setting, planning, and reflecting on the experiences. What goals do students have that the enrichment experiences will help them reach? What planning can students do to ensure that they learn as much as possible from the enrichment experience? Reflecting on the experiences can be accomplished individually or with others, and you might ask yourself questions such as

1. What did I learn as the result of this experience?

2. What will be the next experience in pursuing this interest or developing the talent or expertise?

An important strategy for reflecting is to journal. Thinking about what has been learned is a critical step in becoming a lifelong learner. Isolated experiences without reflection will have minimal impact.

Assessing what is offered by the school to develop various talent areas can be a valuable exercise. An Enrichment Planning Form (see Figure 7) can direct the attention of the faculty to talent and content areas in which the school offers a variety of enrichment opportunities, both in class and in extracurricular options, and to areas in which there are few, if any, offerings. Such an assessment can begin at a faculty meeting. A way to get everyone involved is to post chart paper with the name of each talent area, and then have teachers circulate, adding any opportunities they know exist to develop talent in vocal music, mathematics, leadership, and so forth. The second step of this assessment process is to brainstorm additional opportunities that could be developed and added. The third step is to do long-range planning of opportunities to add to those already provided. In other words, the starting place is to assess what the school currently offers and then plan for the future.

Enrichment Planning Form

I know children who sing the verses of an unwritten song. Unwrap their gifts and you will know them, too.

What are we doing to develop talent in each of the five areas?	What are we doing to develop talent in each of the five areas?
Current	*Future*

1. General Intellectual Ability

2. Specific Academic Ability
   Mathematics

Science

Language Arts

Social Studies

3. Creativity

4. Leadership

5. Visual and Performing Arts
   Visual Art

Music

Drama

Figure 7. Planning for talent development

Within-School Enrichment Opportunities

Academic Teams

At the elementary, middle school, and high school levels, students participate on academic teams coached by educators. These teams offer opportunities to compete with teams from other schools, which provides a positive focus on learning, often becoming a source of school pride.

Academic team has been a great way for me to participate in an extracurricular activity. It's greatly improved my test-taking ability. I get to meet new kids every year, make new friends, and just have fun! On an educational level, I get to learn about new topics I otherwise wouldn't have learned about. Academic team is hard, but it's fun and well worth the effort!

—Maggie Clouse,
ninth grader

Competitions

Competitions are held in many formats, and they offer opportunities for developing strengths and interests to the next levels. Writing, poster, and other art competitions may be submitted for judging; however, other types of competitions require individual or team performances. A spelling or geography competition begins at the local school and proceeds to state, national, and sometimes international levels. Karnes and Riley (1996) have provided contact information for a variety of competitions, some of which are available for young people to apply directly without involvement at the school level.

> *The annual Robot Competition is a successful means for promoting engineering to precollege students. This event gives students a chance to solve a real-world engineering problem. The Robot Competition motivates students by challenging them to build a remotely controlled robot that accomplishes a defined task within a competitive setting. Using only the materials provided, students have 8 weeks to design, develop, and test a robot that can outperform their competitors. During this time, the students experience the same problems, challenges, and breakthroughs that an engineering team encounters when it takes a product to market. In both cases, there are team dynamics, time constraints, material constraints, and pressure from other teams who are trying to solve the same problems.*

—Stacy Wilson,
university professor of engineering

Debate and Forensics

Participating in debate and forensic events builds confidence and provides occasions for students to develop their skills in a variety of performance categories. Debate and forensics provide preparation for many careers, and students develop communication skills that serve them well over their lifetime. These opportunities may be built into the school day or be the focus of extracurricular activities.

> *The most rewarding element of forensics and debate is that they provide students with both intellectual and vocal outlets. Public speaking and debate hone the writing and analytical skills that are necessary for success both in and outside of the classroom. Most of all, forensics reaches out to students at all points of the educational spectrum: from the brightest of children to those who need an extra nudge to keep interested in class. Almost everyone has the ability to talk; however, forensics and debate turn empty words and phrases into carefully formulated and informed arguments that truly allow students to be heard.*

> —Corey Alderdice,
> university senior
> and international award-winning
> participant in forensics and debate

Problem-Solving Programs

Destination ImagiNation (DI), which is open to young people of various ages, is a program with an emphasis on creative problem solving. Two types of challenges are involved in this problem-solving program. The Central Team Challenge is the long-term focus activity, while the Instant Challenge taps the team's ability to solve problems spontaneously. The competition fosters teamwork, divergent thinking, and problem-solving skills. Students also build confidence as they hone their presentation skills.

> *I think Destination ImagiNation is good for anybody who wants to expand his or her mind. D.I. helps you speak in front*

of crowds, builds teamwork, and makes you think outside the box. It is a great experience for everyone!

—Karen Winter,
seventh grader

The Future Problem Solving Program (FPSP) is a six-step model that teaches students to use creative and critical thinking, as well as to think futuristically as they explore challenges and propose plans of action to solve societal problems. Teams of 4th, 5th, and 6th graders (Junior), 7th, 8th, and 9th graders (Middle), and 10th, 11th, and 12th graders (Senior) prepare throughout the year. Teams compete at regional, state, and international levels. Other aspects of FPSP are individual problem solving, action-based problem solving (which is designed for use in the classroom), community problem solving, and scenario writing.

Completing the project of acquiring the money to secure the safety of a deadly curve on Kentucky Highway 146 affected the lives of our community, our school, our team, and our team members individually and personally.

Numerous strangers have approached me and thanked me graciously for what we have done and shared their story of how the road had affected them in such a dreadful way, as it had many of their friends and family. It gave me a great feeling of gratitude and pride to know that my school had pulled off something with this much of a positive impact on all ages in our community to help settle the past and secure the future.

I believe that community problem solving is a good way to get students involved in their community and get your efforts well known. The program itself is what gave us direction to get things accomplished, and the recognition we received helped to get out our hard efforts and encourage other schools to take part in similar efforts. If you can make a difference in one life, then

your efforts are well worthwhile, and it's worth it to tackle the
next problem.

—Becky Nix,
ninth grader

The Odyssey of the Mind Program provides creative problem-solving opportunities for students of various ages. The program involves teams in the pursuit of solutions to long-term problems, and it also fosters individual creativity through the spontaneous part of the program. Because there are several types of problems, the team members can select a long-term problem of interest to them. The competitions are held at regional, state, and international levels.

I, for one, don't know what I would be without this organiza-
tion. I was always a very shy person who hated speaking out in
class. One of my teachers introduced me to the wonderful world
of Odyssey of the Mind, where I have gained self-confidence
and learned to express myself in many different ways. I now
enjoy preparing skits, performing in front of people—includ-
ing my peers—and engaging in problem solving. Through
Odyssey of the Mind I have learned the art of creating costumes
and enjoying my creativity in ways I would never have dreamed
of 2 years ago. I owe my newfound self to being involved in
Odyssey of the Mind. I wish all students could experience the
joy of creativity.

—Bethany Bargo,
sixth grader

Literature-Based Programs

Junior Great Books utilizes a shared-inquiry approach to literature. Students develop critical thinking skills, essential reading skills, and listening skills in addition to speaking and writing skills. Any trained leader, including educators, parents, and volunteers, may facilitate the session. Junior Great Books is fully implemented in some schools as an integral part of their language arts curriculum. However, the program certainly lends itself to in-school or out-of- school enrichment.

> *Using the Junior Great Books program supplements and extends traditional approaches to literacy by employing higher level thinking skills in both reading comprehension and writing. Students are not only encouraged, but also expected to discuss topics in disciplined, freethinking sessions where diversity of thought and opinion is sought in the interpretation of the stories and the authors' intent and style. Students are required to validate their interpretations by finding passages of support in the text, thus teaching students concepts such as identifying problems, supporting details, using inferences, supporting an argument with reasoning and evidence, drawing conclusions, and identifying fact and opinion. All of these reading skills are also then employed in various writing activities that require students to internalize the material and respond to questions and prompts.*

> —Diana Stratton,
> elementary school principal

In Literature Circles, students come together to discuss a book they are reading. Groups may consist of the entire class or only four or five students that have self-selected the same book to read. Both fiction and nonfiction may be used. At first, the teacher leads students with various discussion forms, although students eventually begin to share in natural conversation. A few suggested topics of discussion are the characters' motives, the plot, the book's connections to the students' lives, and the author's style. As discussions continue, students reflect, write, and develop new works related to the reading. Once established, Literature Circles are usually directed by the students and run smoothly.

All students benefit from the variety and empowerment of Literature Circles. Gifted learners benefit greatly. Student book choice allows individuals to select books at appropriate reading levels while pursuing topics and authors of interest. Reading becomes an adventure students enjoy as they search to understand texts at higher levels. Students develop crafty questioning tactics, and self-expression improves. Much needed skills such as researching, analyzing, synthesizing, communicating, creating, and performing are all fostered through Literature Circles. Ask the children involved in Literature Circles why they like it, and they will simply reply, "It's fun!"

—Teresa Vincent,
elementary teacher

Leadership Seminars

Educators plan and offer leadership seminars for students who are interested or talented in leadership. They often use representatives of business and industry who have studied leadership to facilitate these sessions. The focus of leadership seminars is on the content and skills of leadership. For example, communication, planning, and understanding group dynamics are key skills for effective leaders to use. Service learning projects allow young people to hone their leadership skills as they work with others to reach a goal. It is important for leadership seminars to be open to students who are interested in, as well those who are talented in, leadership.

Leadership seminars are a great way for student leaders to share ideas and practice their leadership skills. Elementary students benefit from watching middle and high school student leaders direct group activities and guide breakout sessions at our annual districtwide Leadership Seminar. Older student leaders serve as great mentors for elementary students with leadership potential.

Students have the opportunity to showcase service projects at the Leadership Seminar. Students prepare posters, PowerPoint presentations, and displays to highlight their service projects.

Community leaders are an important resource for leadership seminars. As community leaders tell the story of their leadership journeys, students see themselves and gain encouragement to overcome the obstacles they may encounter. They also are motivated to set leadership goals that will help make our world better.

—Mary Evans,
elementary school principal

Send-Out or Pull-Out Services

The goal of send-out and pull-out services is to provide students challenging learning opportunities with peers who share interests and have similar abilities. The gifted resource teacher knows about gifted and talented children and is familiar with strategies to remove the learning ceiling for them. An art or music specialist or a teacher with a specialization in a core content area may teach send-out or pull-out services.

Being able to participate in a pull-out program provided me with numerous opportunities that would not have been available in a regular classroom. It allowed me to interact with people from other schools with whom I could relate. There were activities that made me think, instead of mindlessly going through the motions. There were lessons on subjects that were not available at my school. Through my pull-out experience, I believe that I gained a greater understanding of certain concepts and expanded my horizons past what was offered to me in a regular classroom.

—Meribeth Hamilton,
university freshman

Simulations

The purpose of a simulation is to create a situation that is as close to reality as possible, yet free of risk. A simulation allows participants to learn from being involved in a real-life situation. Some popular simulations focus on state government, the stock market, and the United Nations.

The Kentucky Youth Assembly (KYA) is a mock state government program operated by the Kentucky YMCA. Its purpose is to allow thousands of middle school and high school students the opportunity to practice state government in action. KYA has given me a greater understanding of others and of myself. No longer is my question "Can I help?," but "How can I help?" KYA provided enrichment to what I learned in school and taught me the importance of relationships, leadership, and service to those who cannot serve themselves. These experiences have shown me the process of our state's government. All of us play an important role in our government, and I have been shown how one voice can make a difference.

—Miriam Muscarella,
ninth grader
and KYA 2003 Governor

Enrichment programs offer many possibilities to children who other-wise may not be exposed to various activities. In some cases, enrichment activities are the first time children can get involved with subjects outside of the school curriculum, such as tennis, gymnastics, chess, or drama. This is a great way for children to "experiment" with some of these activities and see if they like them and might be interested in trying them again. Enrichment programs also can be a way to further boost a child's interest in various activities.

—Micki Simpson,
parent

Clubs and Organizations

Clubs and organizations are offered in communities through various public and private agencies. Knowing what clubs and organizations are available in the area helps young people avail themselves of different opportunities. Clubs and organizations tap a wide range of interests, needs, and abilities, and active participation in such groups may nurture interests and develop talents and skills.

4-H, the youth education branch of the Cooperative Extension Service, strives to assist youth in developing to their full potential. With an emphasis on developing life skills and learning by doing, 4-H assists young people in building character through activities and projects.

> *4-H is no longer all about sows, cows, and plows. For me, it has been an exciting way to bring out leadership qualities in others and myself. I have gained so many special relationships through 4-H that have benefited me on numerous occasions, and, best of all, I have gained lifelong friends. Leaders are working to bring a traditionally domestic and agricultural program into the 21st century by providing opportunities for kids who don't know a thing about horse judging or sowing, but want a chance to develop their talents in leadership and teamwork.*

—Sarah Gill,
university freshman

Both the Boy Scouts of America and Girl Scouts focus on the character development of young people. Designed for children from primary through grade 12, Scouting develops leadership, values, social conscience, and citizenship.

> *Girl Scouts has given me the opportunity to grow as a person and try new things. I've been able to develop leadership, work with younger Scouts and the community, and have fun. Scouts challenges me: I've gone whitewater rafting, skiing, rock climbing, and on high ropes courses. I think Girl Scouts has helped shape me as an individual and helped me become more mature and independent.*

—Katie Pfohl,
12th grader

Book Clubs

Book clubs may be organized by interest in specific types of books or to cultivate interests in reading a range of books. The group may reflect an age group or provide an opportunity to interact with individuals in various grades or ages. The club may choose a book for the group to read and discuss, or it may have each member review and report on a book. Book clubs provide the opportunity to enjoy sharing in a discussion of books and the company of others who enjoy reading.

As a group of well-rounded females, our book club meets once every 5 to 8 weeks. At each session, we open by giving our opinion of the book we had read, such as what we liked or disliked and whether or not we would recommend it to other people. These comments on the book's structure lead to more discussion on the theme and other aspects. Our reading is an eclectic mix, ranging from bestsellers to female-oriented literature.

Being a teenager among a large group of married women in this book club, I felt as though I had the least experience with literature and the world. However, the books we read and discuss allow for people of any level in life to relate. My views on the books we have read may be a little less informed, but the thoughts from all of the women help me view the world from a more adult perspective and allows me to branch my thoughts into more directions.

—Ma'ayan Plaut,
10th grader

Drama, Music, and Art Opportunities

Community groups offer opportunities for children to develop their interests and talents in drama, music, and the arts through events and classes. Students may participate in a youth orchestra or a community band. Art organizations often host exhibits that include categories for the work of young visual artists. Community opportunities in the arts are often featured during the summer and on weekends.

> *Throughout my childhood, I had several opportunities to be involved in the arts. From the age of 5, I enjoyed participating in community theater. The stage was an accepting place for a gawky little girl with a boisterous attitude. I was encouraged to sing, dance, and act, skills that were rarely requested at school. I firmly believe that children should be encouraged to develop their creativity through the arts. After all, I wouldn't be the person I am today without the arts.*
>
> —Julie Roberts,
> kindergarten teacher

Mentorships

Mentors can be teachers, parents, community members, university personnel, or any other person who has the expertise that matches the student's interests. Mentors can meet with the student in person or may communicate via the telephone or the Internet. The most important consideration when planning a mentoring opportunity is the genuine interest and maturity of the student to carry out the pursuit of knowledge. A key consideration when selecting the mentor is his or her commitment to following through when working with the young person.

> *Gifted children have this consuming interest in certain ideas, but their peers aren't ready to take a similar interest in those ideas. Many adults in their lives (parents and teachers) might be able to take such an interest, but frequently they are primarily concerned with the child's moral or social development, worrying whether he or she will be well adjusted or will turn out alright. Gifted kids want and need contact with people who*

are interested in their ideas for their own sake. Without it, they experience a unique—and very acute—kind of loneliness

—Homer White,
university professor of mathematics,
Latin and geometry mentor
to middle school student

Summer Programs

Colleges, universities, art centers, and schools offer summer programs as daytime or residential programs. The benefits of these programs are that they provide opportunities for students to learn challenging materials with others who are equally interested and passionate about the topic of study. Frequently, these summer programs are located on higher education campuses where there are resources that may not be available in elementary, middle, and high schools. Programs vary in length and in emphasis. Two places to find information about summer programs are the Web sites for the National Association for Gifted Children (http://www.nagc.org) and the Duke University Talent Identification Program's (TIP) Educational Opportunity Guide (http://www.tip.duke.edu).

Where to begin? "Life-changing" fits it so well, but is a bit vague. I'll have to go with: The summer programs at Western Kentucky University have allowed me to grow not only intellectually, but also on a personal level. Through the various classes I've learned an amazing amount, and I've made friends that I will keep for life. At the same time, I was able to learn more about who I really am.

—Chris Ginter,
10th grader

Weekend or Saturday Programs

Weekend classes are offered in a variety of content areas, so students can take classes that are of high interest to them. These programs are often held on college and university campuses, offering the advantages of resources that may not be available in schools and promoting postsecondary education by familiarizing students with a campus. These programs can stretch across 4 to 6 weeks, providing the opportunity for hands-on, minds-on learning.

It was early one Saturday morning when I awoke for my first day at college. I wasn't a real college student. I'm still only in the fourth grade, but I was enrolled in a Super Saturday Seminar called "Math + Science = Fun, Fun, Fun" at Western Kentucky University.

We did many interesting activities over the course of the 5-week program. We experimented with bubble gum, Jell-O, and Coke, measuring the sugar content of the various items. We made kaleidoscopes and studied angles. We learned about tessellations and shapes. Each student used a tessellation to design a T-shirt.

I'm glad I had the opportunity to go to the classes. I made new friends and learned new things. College life sure is great when you're only 9 years old!

—Drew Napper,
4th grader

Study Groups

A parent, teacher, or other interested adult gathers a small group of students who share a common interest or goal to engage in a focused study. The purpose can be to learn a foreign language, create a literacy circle, or pursue any topic of interest to the group.

Student-Initiated Projects

Students develop plans about a topic in which they have interest or expertise. Student-initiated projects may impact their school, individuals, or the community. These projects may be one-time events, or they may be ongoing. The student sets a goal and then works with others to carry out the project.

When I was younger, I remember checking my Grandfather's heartbeat. (He had heart problems.) His struggle, which led to his death, made me want to help others. Through my drive and determination, I will get the best possible education needed to prepare myself to be the best doctor possible.

As part of my education, I have studied art from different periods. My mentor encouraged me to conduct an art tour in my house. Finally, an artist friend of ours had a great idea. It was to make a fundraiser out of an art show and use four different homes a year to raise money. These art tours require a great deal of work. I have to find sponsors, prepare docent notes, design and address invitations, and even plan menus.

Donated money goes to different charitable organizations of my choice. I started a fund at the Community Foundation of West Kentucky, and I am the youngest account holder there. The fund is called the "Kelsey Curd Ladt 'Make a Difference' Fund."

—Kelsey Ladt,
age 8

Travel Study

Travel study opportunities allow students to learn as they travel. They provide experiences within the student's home country and abroad. Preparation for the travel experience maximizes the learning, which is shaped by time spent in each place and the focus of the experiences.

Since I have had the privilege of traveling with The Center for Gifted Studies, the world outside small-town Kentucky has come alive. When I see great works of art in a textbook, when I hear about important world events, when I read a great novel, I now make heart and mind connections with those pictures and words. I can see the British people and the Italian churches and Renaissance art and taste the French cooking.

—Scottie Beth Fleming,
12th grader

Conclusion

This publication has described enrichment opportunities that go above and beyond the regular curriculum, as well as programs and services that spark interests and develop skills and expertise both within the school or beyond in the local or broader community. The key to effective enrichment is matching opportunities to individual needs, interests, and abilities. When the match occurs, wonderful possibilities are available to encourage learning at high levels. The rich array of enrichment opportunities can develop lifelong learners.

Resources

Web Sites

4-H
http://www.4-h.org

The youth education branch of the Cooperative Extension Service, 4-H strives to assist youth in developing to their fullest potential. With an emphasis on developing life skills and learning by doing, 4-H assists young people in building character through activities and projects.

American Forensics Association
http://www.americanforensics.org

This professional association for teachers of forensics provides information ranging from listing of forensic competitions to professional development opportunities.

Boy Scouts of America and Girl Scouts of the USA
http://www.scouting.org
http://www.girlscouts.org

Both the Boy Scouts of America and Girl Scouts of the USA focus on the character development of young people. Designed for children from primary through grade 12, Scouting develops leadership, values, social conscience, and citizenship.

The Center for Gifted Studies
at Western Kentucky University
http://www.wku.edu/gifted

The Center has provided opportunities for gifted and talented young people, their parents, and their educators for more than 20 years.

Destination ImagiNation
http://www.destinationimagination.org

Emphasizing creativity, problem solving, and team building, Destination ImagiNation poses situations that challenge participants to use skills in innovative ways. This international competition boasts two types of challenges: One takes teams months to prepare, while the other is improvisation.

Educational Opportunity Guide:
A Directory of Programs for the Gifted
http://www.tip.duke.edu

Duke University's Talent Identification Program (TIP) offers information and opportunities for gifted young people. Not only can participants use test results to help assess their abilities, but they also receive invaluable information regarding enrichment, study, and travel possibilities. TIP's Educational Opportunity Guide lists hundreds of year-round and seasonal programs.

Future Problem Solving Program

http://www.fpsp.org

The Future Problem Solving Program (FPSP) encourages and develops creative and critical thinking as young people find solutions to real problems. FPSP can be either competitive or not, curricular or extracurricular. The goal is to empower students with creative problem-solving skills.

Junior Great Books

http://www.greatbooks.org

Junior Great Books utilizes a shared-inquiry approach to literature. Students develop critical thinking skills, essential reading skills, and listening skills in addition to speaking and writing skills.

Kentucky Youth Assembly

http://www.kyianaymcas.org

Sponsored by the YMCA, the Kentucky Youth Assembly (KYA) encourages young people to learn how government works; debate topics of local, state, and national interest; and make friendships with future leaders.

MathCounts

http://www.mathcounts.org

Middle school "matheletes" compete as a team or individually in the "sport" of mathematics. This national program encourages achievement in math through competitions under a coach's tutelage. The program has received multiple Presidential commendations.

National Association for Gifted Children
http://www.nagc.org

The National Association for Gifted Children (NAGC) is a nonprofit organization designed to advocate for young people who are gifted and talented. NAGC serves as the control central in the field of gifted education.

National Mentoring Partnership
http://www.mentoring.org

The National Mentoring Partnership provides information and resources for people interested in mentoring. From information on how to become a mentor to how to find one, this site offers practical advice and invaluable strategies—even funding sources.

Prisoners of Time
http://www.ed.gov/pubs/PrisonersOfTime/PoTSchool/index.html

After 2 years of research, the National Education Commission on Time and Learning published this report that examined the constraints time places on the American education system. The premise of the report argued that the current 180-day, 6-hours-a-day instruction is the "design flaw" of education. The Commission proposed a longer school day with flexible hours to meet individual needs.

National Geography Bee
http://www.nationalgeographic.com/geographybee

Sponsored by the National Geographic Society, this program encourages interest and enthusiasm in geography for children in grades 4–8. Thousands of students compete each year, with winners meeting in Washington, DC, hoping to win the $25,000 grand prize.

Odyssey of the Mind
http://www.odysseyofthemind.com

Odyssey of the Mind encourages creative problem solving in students from kindergarten through college. Working in teams, participants develop their creativity as they solve open-ended problems. Teams come from more than 25 countries for the championship.

The Curriculum Project
http://www.curriculumproject.com

Based on types of learning, the guides available from The Curriculum Project provide a variety of product ideas, including the main attributes of each.

Robot Competitions
http://www.robots.net/rcfaq.html

This site lists robotic competitions held throughout the world, plus answers to frequently asked questions.

Road Map for National Security: Imperative for Change
http://www.nssg.gov/PhaseIIIFR.pdf

Published before 9/11, this federal report emphasizes the steps that must be taken in order to maintain national security. Educating on high levels is a main emphasis.

Venn Diagrams
http://www.venndiagram.com

Although originally designed for the corporate world, this Web site includes numerous educational examples and templates of Venn Diagrams, including those with multiple circles to encourage higher level thinking.

References

Coleman, L. J., & Cross, T. L. (2001). *Being gifted in school: An introduction to development, guidance, and teaching.* Waco, TX: Prufrock Press.

Curry, J., & Samara, J. (1994). *Developing units for primary students.* Bowling Green: Kentucky Association for Gifted Education.

Kanevsky, L. (2003, Summer). Tiering with Venn diagrams. *Gifted Education Communicator,* 42–44.

Karnes, F. A., & Stephens, K. R. (2000). *The ultimate guide to student product development and evaluation.* Waco, TX: Prufrock Press.

Karnes, F. A., & Riley, T. L. (1996). *Competitions: Maximizing your abilities.* Waco, TX: Prufrock Press.

National Education Commission on Time and Learning. (1994). *Prisoners of time.* Washington, DC: Author.

Renzulli, J. S., & Reis, S. M. (1997). *The schoolwide enrichment model: A how-to guide for educational excellence* (2nd ed.). Mansfield Center, CT: Creative Learning Press.

Schiever, S. W., & Maker, C. J. (2003). New directions in enrichment and acceleration. In N. Colangelo & G. A. Davis (Eds.), *Handbook of gifted education* (3rd ed., pp. 163–173). Boston: Allyn and Bacon.

U.S. Commission on National Security for the 21st Century. (2001). *Road map for national security: Imperative for change.* Retrieved April 15, 2004, from http://www.nssg.gov/PhaseIIIFR.pdf

Julia Link Roberts is the Mahurin Professor of Gifted Studies and director of The Center for Gifted Studies at Western Kentucky University. In 1998, Dr. Roberts was named a Distinguished Professor at Western Kentucky University. She was honored in 2001 as the first recipient of the National Association for Gifted Children's David W. Belin Advocacy Award, and she was selected for inclusion in *Profiles of Influence in Gifted Education: Historical Perspectives and Future Directions* (2003). Dr. Roberts serves on the boards of the National Association for Gifted Children, the Kentucky Association for Gifted Education, and *Gifted Child Today*. She also is a member the Governor's Advisory Council for the Gifted and Talented in Kentucky. Dr. Roberts is founder of The Center for Gifted Studies, which offers programs for children and young people, parents, and educators. In 2001, The Center for Gifted Studies celebrated its 20th year. She received her bachelor's degree at the University of Missouri and her Ed.D. at Oklahoma State University.

Printed in the United States
by Baker & Taylor Publisher Services